Camden Publishing House,

Kangeta Town,

P. O. Box 577, 60600

Maua, Meru County,

KENYA.

Copyright @ 2021 by Tarcisio F. B. Gichunge

All rights are reserved. No part of this book may be reproduced, stored in a retrieval system, or transcribed in whatsoever form, or by any means, electronic, mechanical, photocopying, recording or otherwise, without the prior written consent of the publisher.

Edited, authored and published by Camden Publishing House, Kangeta Town, in Meru County, Kenya.

TABLE OF CONTENTS

About the author
Introduction

Chapter One

1.0 How tribalism was planted in Kenya
1.1 When fields of tribalism were manured
1.2 When Kenya harvested fruits of tribalism
1.3 Invention of Harambee Spirit in Kenya
1.4 Jomo Kenyatta bequeathed Harambee Legacy

Chapter Two
2.0 Forerunners of tribalism in Kenya

Chapter Three
3.0 How colonialists planted tribalism in Kenya
3.1 Waswahili were new products in Kenya
3.2 Waswahili are products of Ameru
3.3 A new theory of Ameru and Waswahili

Chapter Four
4.0 Challenge to the Historians
4.1 Where did Arabs export their slaves to?

Chapter Five
5.0 Creation of Kenyan tribes
5.1 Meaning of Bura, Kora and Tulla

Chapter Six
6.0 How tribalism was confirmed in Kenya
6.1 Politicians' craftiness in deals
6.2 Beyond tribalism thinking by Kenyans

HISTORY OF KENYA BEFORE AND AFTER COLONIZATION

About the Author: Mr. Tarcisio F. B. Gichunge

Mr. Tarcisio Francis Baimaana Gichunge was born on 25th, August 1946 in Njia Location, Igembe Central Sub County, of Meru County, Kenya. He attended Kaongo Kamau Primary School and sat for Competitive Entrance Examination in 1959 under Index No. AE/859, and passed to enter Tuuru Intermediate School in 1960, after which he passed KPE Examination in 1962 and enrolled at Nkubu High School in January 1963. In 1966, he sat for

Cambridge School Certificate Examination and passed with credits.

He joined the Civil Service in 1967 and worked in various Government Ministries up to July 2001 when he retired as a Senior District Personnel Officer on attaining the mandatory age of 55 years.

While in the public service, he had attended various Professional courses at GTI Maseno, GTI Mombasa and Bandari College Mombasa and KIA Kabete, Nairobi, Kenya finalizing his career as a Certified Public Secretary CPS (K) finalist in 1983 and Chief Personnel Officer. He later attended The University of Pittsburgh, Pennsylvania, USA in 1990 for a Postgraduate Diploma in Human Resource and Personnel Management and specialized in IFMIS Program for Payroll Data Management.

Before his retirement from the public service, he had served as a member of the Board of Management of various Secondary Schools, among them Kilima Mungu Girls' Secondary School and Kangeta Girls' Secondary School where he had served for 25 years. After retirement, he enrolled with The Writers'

Bureau London to acquire writing and editing skills specializing as an author of books. He is now a Published Author of seventy two books, including this one.

His other books' titles are:

1. Fate of Souls

2. Biography of Father Francesco Soldati

3. Blessings and curses in the African Tradition

4. Always say Thank you my God

5. Be good leaders for remembrance

6. Attitude towards theft of Public Funds

7. Consider your Purpose in life

8. Democracy is an Illusion

9. Era of Consolata Missionaries in Igembe, Kenya

10. God Avenges Evil and Rewards Good

11. Follow Your Stars in Life

12. Honor your Father and Mother

13. in the Footsteps of Father Francesco Soldati

14. Kimeru Myths and Legends

16. Kimeru Proverbs, Legends and Njuno

17. Know your people, else you will marry your sister

18. Live Good Life in God's Name

19. Live Well according to God's Will

20. Live Well with God's People

21. Meru National Park: The Unsung Glory

22. Meru Origins, customs, culture and traditions

23. Motivational Talk for Success

24. Planting Evil and Ruining Your Destiny

25. Positive Thinking is Your Success

26. Positive Attitude: Unity of the Universe

27. Prepare how you will die

28. Walking in Kenyan History and Ameru Cultural Anthropology

29. Historic Journey of Ameru and their Cultural Anthropology

30. We all pray for Enviable Death

31. What makes you tick in Life!

32. When God Tempts You

33. When Kenya Said No to Impunity

34. Where Only Eagles Dare

35. Why Leaders never appreciate others

36. Why Leaders never Breed Leaders

37. Why Meru People Crossed the Red Sea

38. You and Your God; Moral Theology

39. You Reap What You Plant

40. Why Kenyans are not Historians

41. Biography of Senior Chief Daniel M'Iringo Kiringo - 2 series

42. The Benefits of Education Transformation

43. Transformation and Living in Future

44. Very poor, but Very Rich

45. Biography of Bro Giuseppe Argese of Mukululu Shrine

46. Walking in Kenyan History

47. Ameru Cultural Anthropology

48. Ameru and their Fragmented Democracy

49. Beware: Traditional Curses are real and biting

50. Biography of M'Mwothiru and Kathika Families

51. Do not Deny Young Kenyans Information

52. Civic Education for Young People

53. Youth are the Salt of the Country; A Perspective

54. Making Informed and Effective Choices - 2 series

55. Families Should Avoid Sitting on Curses

56. Americans Hoyee and Congratulations from Kenya

57. Heroes and Heroines of Meru History

58. For God's sake, keep Kenya's Unity

59. Lake Maggado Igombe Epic Crater of Meru

60. The Life That We Live

61. Why most people should be Writers

62. Miraa History in Meru and its legislation in Kenya

63. Autobiography of Tarcisio Gichunge

64. Parents may abandon you, but the Lord...

65. African social therapists and psychic shepherds

66. Epochs of Ameru in History expounded

67. Ameru groomed their leaders from childhood

68. When a girl was born in Meru, Kenya

69. How Colonizers crafted tribalism in Kenya

70. How Harambee Spirit was curtailed in Kenya

71. Trusting in my Guardian Angels

72. History of Kenya before and after colonization

Introduction

HISTORY OF KENYA BEFORE AND AFTER COLONIZATION

By Gichunge WA M'Thirua

In any civilization, society and community, young people are expected to be partakers, contributors and participants in the future development of their nation. Therefore, excluding young people from the knowledge regarding their expectations, prospects, potentials, opportunities, outlooks, hopes and beliefs is the worst mistake a generation could be subjected to by those in control and leadership.

Denying young people information by whoever is irresponsible, again the most grievous and obvious crime a generation can come upon and run into from the older generation. Generations in humanity are existent by an act of God in order that they may pass knowledge to generation after generation.

If a generation fails in its duty to pass good information to the upcoming generation, then the default generation will bear the pain of a revenge from God who is the avenger of all evil doings.

Long ago, Kenyans were divided along their Kenyan tribes by the colonial masters who used the "divide and rule" technique and tactic to divide them, but today Kenyans are Kenyans as one tribe, especially when they tackle their national problems and issues. During the colonial era Kenyans were silently divided along the lines of tribalism imposed upon them by the colonizers in order to simplify their administrative process. The first tool that the colonizers used to contain tribalism was the appointment of Tribal Chiefs and District Commissioners who remained very loyal and powerful even after Kenya's Independence in December 1963.

Through the Chiefs' Authority Act of 1920's, the people of Kenya were subdued and bundled into their Sub Locations, Locations and Districts after the introduction of Kipande System of Administration and Limitation of Movement (Kisalimo). That system required the natives to carry an Identification Card to prove and confirm their Locations in addition to giving the name of their tribe into which they belonged before they would be allowed to travel to the next Location of residence. Thus, the Kipande was meant to identify the tribe into which the holder belonged and where he resided. The system was also meant to identify and punish those who broke the laws of the colony by imprisoning them in their home areas or localities. Kipande long ago was used to record the negative activities of the holder in order to be aware of the person one could trust or not trust. Communities were also identified by their customs and culture, where young people were taught what was good and what was bad in their communities.

Young people therefore, grew up in knowledge of what was good and what was bad in their community. The communities knew their leaders including when they were expected to replace them without delays when time matured for their replacements. Leadership was not for any Tom, Dick and Harry, hence in those days, there was no politicking about positions because leaders had already emerged and their names had been noted and passed over to Mugwe (The Judiciary) for confirmation (swearing-in) during the day of NTUIKO festivities and celebrations for the hand-over of public duties witnessed by the communities.

Ameru people lived in Mboa (Manda Island) Kenya from AD 1000 after their arrival from Egypt up to the day they were disturbed by the Nguuntune (the

Portuguese) while being hunted down as slaves where they practiced democracy in their community even before colonizers arrived in Kenya. Kenya had communities which had long history from long ago and Ameru are among such communities who had long history. In Kenya Ameru lived and practiced democracy long before the arrival of Europeans.

Ameru people concentrated in their affairs and left the matters of the leadership to those who were blessed with leadership traits and qualities to take over their respective leadership positions without unnecessary competitions. Leadership in those days did not bring wealth into the families, instead it would entice and attract curses and nobody therefore aspired to be a leader in the community, instead, wise people avoided leadership and agreed to be led by those who volunteered to be cursed by the publics who never appreciated the actions of their leaders a hundred per cent. Leadership was a burden placed upon leaders by the people who expected to curse leaders for bad leadership in the end if they did not perform well.

Long ago, communities gathered to curse their leaders, but they never gathered to bless them when they performed well. Communities were quick to notice the wrongdoings of their leaders but they never appreciated their good performance and that is why many wise people never aspired for leadership positions in their communities. Today, leaders are insensitive to blasphemies, spells, jinxes and curses from their communities and that is why "no leader has ever bred another good leader from his family except for a single case that people can quote among millions." In this case, we can quote Bush Family in USA, as a blessed family. When that happens, it is by God's grace, but it never goes beyond a few generations. Why? It is because of what people came to embrace as politics, that every Tom, Dick and Harry can lead people because leadership is never a burden but a source of wealth in today's world.

Long ago, families used to breed good leaders within their families because they continued to receive blessings from God in their good and exemplary leadership. God confirms good leadership by breeding good leaders within the families but (God out of His will), condemns bad leadership by denying families' leadership inheritance and succession (that is why you will never hear sons or daughters of past leaders being actively involved in their fathers' role of politics). Bad leaders never breed leaders (because of curses) in their families and because leadership traits and qualities fade away from the families within one generation of bad leadership (through curses that they carry into their homes).

However, when Kenya became Independent in December 1963, Mzee Jomo Kenyatta immediately embraced politics of the Kenyan communities which recognized the problems of the people as illiteracy, poverty and ignorance which faced all Kenyans as one tribe called Kenyans. At Independence, Kenya had five races that were recognized as Africans, Arabs, Asians, Europeans and other mixed people who had come from other continents though not as tribes that were completely distinct from the races.

In Kenya lived the communities but not tribes and today Kenyans have appreciated living in Counties which compose their communities as residents. In Counties people live without talking about tribes and therefore people talk about their Counties and their residents. People talk about development issues in their Counties and not people who reside there. Kenyans are coming back to their senses, that if you live in Samburu, you would like development to go to Samburu County while ignoring the fact of where you come from.

Voting where you are the resident is a good sign of development consciousness in residence. People like development in their areas of residence!

CHAPTER ONE

1.0 HOW TRIBALISM WAS PLANTED IN KENYA

When the colonialists arrived in Kenya, they found Kenyans living in their respective areas of settlements. Kenyans did not know what tribe they belonged but simply people knew and acknowledged that they lived in Meruland, Kikuyuland, Luoland, Luyhialand, Kisiiland, Kambaland, Masailand, Turkanaland, Taitaland, Giriamaland, Durumaland, Pokomoland, Garissaland, Manderaland, Nandiland, Kipsigisland, Embuland and so forth. People lived in Kenya in their respective homes and villages without names of tribes. It is the colonizer who introduced the names of tribes for his own convenience for governance. Kenyans readily accepted the names of baptism without water and the Holy Spirit.

Thus, tribalism was planted in Kenya by the colonizer without water and the Holy Spirit and that is why tribalism is not a blessing but something unwanted, undesirable and unwelcome in Kenya. Kenyans had lived with tribalism being suppressed in the colonial era, but as soon as Kenya gained independence, people started to feel the weight and burden of tribalism in the name of marginalization of one settlement area or tribe by those in power. People started complaining about marginalization as part of tribalism because those in power started to control resources which needed to be shared by the communities equitably and fairly by the leaders. Then who is who, came into play.

Why did that happen? It is because of shared economic, social and political interests. People long ago lived in their villages without sharing anything. People never shared wealth, social interests or politics. People lived their own lives without bothering others. They lived like animals in the wilderness. But now that people are forced to share the resources and as a result conflicts are bound to be, but the question of tribalism should not arise where communities live in harmony under good leaders.

1.1 WHEN FIELDS OF TRIBALISM WERE MANURED

When Kenyans elected their leaders for the first time after Independence to represent them in their constituencies, they also agreed to share their wealth, social interests and political interests. They also agreed to weed out the weed that had affected their freedom since the days of colonization. Much later, Kenyans accepted to weed out their fields of tribalism once every five years through a General Election of their leaders. Every tribal area was required to produce their leaders to ensure that communities represented were well catered for through shared development projects that took place in their constituencies.

The elected leaders became the supervisors in their respective fields of representation but not implementers of the projects. But later, the supervisors out of their own volition and craftiness assumed the extra powers beyond that of a supervisor to become the senior managers who would award contracts and pay the workers through a CDF Kitty controlled by their cronies (since they were their servants having elected them). The supervisor over the years, after assuming the role of the senior manager today, directs who the contractors should be and should not be. That way, the process of tribalism has been sealed in a certain community through the leaders who become spokesmen of the communities.

Because of the power of controlling the resources, the leaders therefore, started talking about their people as "if they owned people" the source of their power. From that point, the elected leaders fooled the masses to follow them through (carrot stick trick) the power of what money can buy including the power itself. With power the people's spoken because they control the resources.

When leaders are given the chance of spokesmen for their communities, they go ahead to speak for the communities as tribes and therefore confirming the position of tribalism in Kenya. Kenyan leaders have become real tribalists because they cannot shout and yell any appeal to the communities without mentioning "my people" as if they are fathers of everybody. Those fellows are not fathers of every reasonable person in Kenya, save for their own children.

When leaders were allowed and passed laws to implement projects in their areas instead of supervising the implementation by the independent implementing agencies, another deal was made and sealed to manure and fertilize tribalism through the elected leaders who were also spokesmen of their tribes. Once the system had been established, the leaders increased in numbers in the fields to enjoy the benefits of the communities' ignorance. They also appointed their cronies to help them manure the fields of tribalism and plundering of public funds meant for the communities' projects in the name of "my people are suffering."

After the communities vote in their leaders, the leaders instead of helping the people, they steal public funds meant for public projects. After every five years, they repeat the same mistake of electing other useless leaders hoping to get better services with the next crop of leaders. Hence, it has become a decent routine of exchanging their leaders as one would change a shirt or a blouse when it becomes dirty! Truly, as one said, Politics is a dirty game and those who play that game are also dirty. Would you believe that "politics has never spared anyone a good name?" That is because it is a dirty game.

1.2 WHEN KENYA HARVESTED FRUITS OF TRIBALISM

Tribalism matured in Kenya when the communities went into the General Elections to elect their leaders in the name of "Constituent Leaders" in December 1969. For the first time, Kenyans were represented in Parliament by their Members of Parliament who spoke on behalf of their communities. Little did people know that in their future, that those leaders would one day speak tribal words! People had never visualized that those leaders would one day speak the way they speak these days.

Leaders speak as if every resident in their Constituencies is in their pockets. They overlook the fact that they speak on behalf of some people who are more intelligent, wealthier, brainier, smarter, more bright, more gifted and knowledgeable but they cannot speak for the communities because they have never aspired or desired that "cursed responsibility." It is cursed because if one fails to fulfill the mandate, he goes home to stamp his family with a curse rubber stamp.

People regard 1969 as the first full and genuine General Elections in Kenya, though not the first Parliament. It was an election that was conducted with full present-day Counties of Kenya represented in the National Assembly of Kenya. Previously, representation did not fully cover the 42 Counties of Kenya in those days. However, after 1969 General Elections several Constituencies were created to cater for the smaller communities which felt left out in the representation.

By 1974 August General Elections, leaders were sober and they spoke reasonably about projects taking place in their areas as they fully appreciated the Government efforts to develop the growing nation. Leaders were honest in their utterances in those years and corruption was unknown.

In December 1979 General Elections, the people went into the elections with a notion of Peace, Love and Unity, because after the death of the Founder of the Harambee Spirit who had died on 22nd, August 1978. People started to experience the emptiness of the Harambee Spirit in their lives soon after the death of President Jomo Kenyatta who had inspired people to embrace the Harambee Spirit.

In September 1983 General Elections, the people were empty and solvent in their hearts because the Harambee Spirit was low in their hearts and souls. People envisioned that Harambee Spirit was in its low spirits and they thought it would never rise again. But President Moi in his Peace, Love and Unity Philosophy proved a true follower of Kenyatta's footsteps of Harambee Nyayo. It is then, that Nyayo Hospital Wards were initiated by President Moi to prove that Kenyans were still together in the Harambee Spirit. In 1984/85 Hospitals like Embu benefited out of Nyayo Wards' forced contributions from the Civil Servants. It was all in view of proving that "Harambee and Nyayo" were in tandem and agreement with Government efforts to develop the nation.

President Daniel arap Moi, embraced the Harambee Spirit which endeared him to the people throughout his 24 years as the President of Kenya. During Moi Presidency, Harambee Spirit was embraced by the rich and poor people. People travelled from one county to another to attend Harambee functions as they embraced brotherhood.

In March 1988, Mlolongo General Elections, many political giants fell out and it appeared as if Mlolongo was meant to push out some leaders who were easily eliminated in the Mlolongo. Many leaders fought against Mlolongo and later it was ignored and abolished with many crying foul about it while claiming that the voters had been bought in advance and before appearing in Mlolongo. Here the bribing of voters appeared for the first time.

In December 1992 General Elections, people went into the elections with some regions crying wolf (tribal clashes) in some Constituencies, for example "Miteitei Clashes" in the Rift Valley. Those clashes became the first bitter fruits of tribalism that Kenyans tasted since Independence in 1963. Nyayo Era spent much of its efforts to counter those clashes for the better part of its administration, while championing Peace, Love and Unity which threatened and out of control within the nation.

By December 1997 General Elections, people had been confused by what politicians called Multi-party elections where even Parliament had divided itself into different groups of politicians through IPPG (Inter Parliamentary Party Groups) which sought to wrestle power from the Executive and to amend the Constitution without a Referendum.

By December 2002, Kenyans had become brave enough to challenge the Executive powers which had formed the habit of detaining dissidents without trial. When Kenyans went into the General Elections on 29th, December 2002, KANU Party was relieved of leadership burden to lead the country after 39 years since 1963. President Mwai Kibaki was sworn-in under NARC (National Rainbow Coalition) Party. Kenyans felt as if they had been born again for defeating KANU Party leadership that they perceived had oppressed the people.

Here, was when people should have learnt, that Parties do not matter in choosing their leaders. They should have learnt that it was not the Manifestos that mattered in choosing leaders. Well prepared Manifestos without good leadership are nothing compared to good leadership without Manifestos. Kibaki was propelled into the General Elections in 2002 almost without a Manifesto, but he became the most successful President in Kenya on being accepted as "Kibaki Tosha" campaign.

He revived a down-trodden economy and achieved a National Percapita Growth of almost 7% by the time of his retirement in March 2013. Kibaki Presidency of good ten years delivered to the Kenyans a brand new Constitution on 27th, August 2010. It is this same Constitution that a few people were clamoring for a change in 2021 through BBI, the effort (it was an effort because two opposing leaders who sat down alone and came up with the idea of Changing the Constitution) of only two warring leaders in Kenya. The effort failed to beat time for 2022 General Elections while its authors were never ashamed.

One credit for the Nyayo Era is that, it brought people together with the Harambee Spirit. Nyayo Era never discouraged the Harambee Spirit. People were united by the Legacy of Harambee Spirit bequeathed by Mzee Jomo Kenyatta. Harambee Spirit had played its part to eradicate and bury tribalism in the deepest grave. With Harambee Spirit, people were impelled to live like Kenyans when they moved from one place to another place in Kenya to attend Harambee Days on Saturdays for worthy causes of their friends without distinction. The Harambee Spirit had made Kenyans live as Kenyans without remembering their communities because they were united by Harambee Spirit.

Kenyans had adopted a new way of life together when visitors from Kisumu, Migori, Kisii, Kuria, Siaya, Busia, Bungoma, Kakamega, Kericho, Nandi, Kitale, Eldoret, Kapenguria, Lodwar, Kapsokwony, Kajiado, Narok, Nyandarwa, Nyeri, Murang'a, Embu, Machakos, Kitui, Taita, Taveta, Kilifi, Kwale, Mandera, Isiolo, Samburu, Marsabit and elsewhere used to spend their nights in Meru or elsewhere after attending the Harambee for their friends. People mingled for love of one another in those days of Harambees. Tribalism had faded in Kenya in those days. Woe to those who clasped Harambee Spirit effort!

That movement and effect of people coming together to attend Harambees in villages throughout Kenya was a motivator and an encouragement for the people to forget tribalism. When Harambee Spirit was slackened by the politicians during Kibaki's Presidency, it was when MPs falsely claimed in Parliament that politicians were barred from attending Harambees as that was being construed as a bribe to the voters in future. From that time MPs evaded the routine of being invited as Guests of Honor in the Harambee functions. That way, they killed the Harambee Spirit in Kenya.

Parliament also clasped the people's effort of helping those in need when sometimes back it was declared that Harambees were banned when General Elections were nearing. You can imagine when a needy person got sick during the General Elections period! The person was bound to die because of the campaigns. God forbid it.

When that happened, MPs detached themselves from the Harambee functions on the grounds that donating in Harambees was a bribe to the voters in the future elections. That excuse discouraged well-wishers from visiting far villages in the country to familiarize themselves with other citizens in Kenya. Familiarization brought people together as Kenyans and not tribalists. Kenyans have suffered the blow and bitter fruits of tribalism since the curtailment of the Harambee Spirit by politicians.

Tribalism is an enemy of Kenyans irrespective of status, place of residence, distance, position, attachment or habitation. When Kenyans were denied the Harambee Spirit by the politicians, they retreated back into their backyards and villages where they were confined as tribalists from their respective homes who never crossed their Constituency borders to attend any Harambee function of which they were ued to in their past.

1.3 INVENTION OF HARAMBEE SPIRIT IN KENYA

Jomo Kenyatta had given a blind eye to tribalism which never existed and did not feature as a problem of the citizens, though the colonizers were aware that they had cunningly designed tribalism within the country and it was only a matter of time that it would explode in their faces. Colonialists knew too well that tribalism is bad and yet they planted its seed in Kenya. They planted tribalism in Kenya and they weeded it and tidied its fields as they manured its farms and they harvested the fruits of tribalism before they left Kenya in December 1963. They left Kenya to suffer the consequences of tribalism that they had cunningly designed over nearly seventy years of their era.

Mzee Jomo Kenyatta invented and devised HARAMBEE SPIRIT to fight illiteracy, poverty and ignorance countrywide. Meanwhile, he ignored tribalism "in-making" since it was non-existent in people's minds during the colonial era, though it became noticeable many years after Independence. Harambee Spirit was an invention of Mzee Jomo Kenyatta, a man who had learnt the spirit of African Nationalism and Socialism from other African leaders who studied and lived in London in 1940's. Jomo Kenyatta was imprisoned in 1953 for seven years and was released from detention under the pressure of all Kenyans among them an individual Jaramogi Oginga Odinga who spearheaded the spirit of Kenyans as one community at the time in order to release Jomo Kenyatta from prison.

Kenyans were united during the colonial era and they spoke one language that of "Independent Kenya." Only the colonizers who preached tribalism because they wanted to divide people for their own advantage and convenience. Jaramogi Oginga Odinga was always in the forefront for the release of Jomo Kenyatta from prison. It was him who also suggested the name of Jomo Kenyatta for Prime Minister in Lancaster Independence talks.

In those days, Kenyans had no knowledge of tribes during the colonial era even though the colonizer had used the "divide and rule tactics" to suppress them. The natives as they were known by the time, always appreciated each other as people from their different villages and not as people from this or that tribe. Today, tribalism is a monster and a creature of post-independent Kenya, where leaders are bedeviled by the usual "tribalistic routine of my people are suffering."

That Harambee Spirit spurred all leaders and Kenyans into development efforts throughout Kenyatta's 15 years' Presidency from 1963 to 1978, when people realized that pulling together would eradicate poverty, illiteracy and ignorance. By 1978, when President Kenyatta died, Kenya had advanced and developed to the stage of "a developing country" in the world away from those countries classified as "poor countries in the world." It was during the Era of Kenya's Harambee Spirit that Kenya advanced from a poor country to a developing country. Jomo Kenyatta never tolerated tribalism in Kenya and his first Cabinet of 15 experienced and honest members was composed of high caliber persons from all regions of Kenya though it ignored some parts of the country for his personal reasons.

1.4 JOMO KENYATTA BEQUEATHED HARAMBEE LEGACY

Mzee Jomo Kenyatta out of his intelligence and wisdom therefore, bequeathed Kenyans a legacy, the HARAMBEE SPIRIT OF UNITY. It is that Legacy which our young generations have not been engaged to learn and to be active about. Most of the current leaders in 2000's and 2020's are the products of the Harambee Spirit in Kenya before it was curtailed by President Kibaki's "selfish-Parliaments." President Kibaki had nothing to do with it. Only Parliamentarians felt the weight of helping the needy. Uhuru Kenyatta Presidency did allow the last nail to be hammered to the Harambee Spirit coffin because he totally ignored Harambee functions.

But if young people were coached about the Harambee Spirit and the history of Harambee, they would grow up in the knowledge that the "Spirit of Harambee" will never tempt or entice them to steal from the public coffers because "pulling together" is a development effort for all. Young leaders would grow knowing that those who steal from the public coffers are the enemies of development in their communities. Well-intentioned people never steal from the public coffers to which they are required to build through their honest contributions.

This book explains how the citizens struggled to develop their nation under the leadership of their committed and dedicated leaders who earnestly tried to understand the full meaning of Democracy. Democracy meant honest and hard work to strengthen their economy in order to enjoy communal social benefits derived from a thriving economy.

But democracy still remained an illusion to them as much as it is today! Tribalism was an illusion in those days but today it has haunted people to the very marrow of their bones as an immutable monster that has terrified every vulnerable and defenseless person in the community. The ignorance of what was Democracy by our past leaders is elucidated in another of our books titled "DEMOCRACY IS AN ILLUSION" by Tarcisio F.B. Gichunge in Amazon.com, which should be read as a comparison to this edition.

In the African culture, customs and traditions, leaders were supposed to be men of honor, blameless and above reproach in life. They were more or less the angels on earth. If any bit of blame was pitted and pocked against them, they exited and vanished from their leadership positions without necessitating a call for their resignation. They resigned voluntarily before being exposed to the grit and gravel with their bare feet! They went into the bottom depth of oblivion where no one ever remembered them again. They became the rotten eggs before hatch!

Today, all leaders without an exception are deaf to many justified calls made against them for their evil deeds. They become deaf because corruption has impinged and affected their hearts, such that the more noise from the community, the harder their skins become in absorbing and engrossing evil into their lives. Thus, leaders have modified and tuned to the wavelength to live evil lives of fear for their activities. They erect high walls in their homes for their protection because they fear their neighbors instead of embracing them for safety. Total insanity!

These days, leaders have no advisers because they think that "leadership is an automatic wisdom distributor and dispenser." The world and villages have advisors, but there are no people to take advice seriously. Ordinary people and leaders take advice for granted either because they are ignorant or because they have no time for listening to the advisors. Those who need advice most, are the ones who reject advisors most of the time. Instead of listening to the advisors, they have always listened to their wives in their bedrooms as their best advisors. Bad leaders have always rejected or ignored advice from those who would have helped them to make good decisions for their communities.

Today, leaders need advice more than anyone else, but unfortunately those leaders think that they are their own advisors because they are "know it all" in their bedrooms with their wives in every matter that concerns their communities. They always assume that an election made them wiser than all those who elected them to their positions. Politicians assume and acquire all intelligence overnight after the election date. They also become encouraged to study and acquire academic excellence overnight because money is "mfunja mlima" and would buy them intelligence which they lacked in their poor backgrounds when they scored only "EEs" in their examinations. To them today, "money is the crusher of hills" or money can acquire anything save for life which no one has ever tried to buy with "dirty or even clean money."

Long ago, advisors were hired and kept in the leaders' courts. Their expense was catered for by the subjects who benefited from their advice because good leaders were assets for the community. That is why even today, advisors and lawmakers are paid through public funds. The only problem is that today leaders have become corrupt in appointments of good advisors, where instead they appoint those who sing their tunes since they are related to them or are cronies in their ideological mentality.

In another book, we have recorded the leaders' activities in Kenya from 1900's to the present time and if you examine those activities deeply, you will make your own conclusions about the leaders' behavior. Bad leaders appoint cronies and incompetent advisors who serve their interests instead of serving the public interests. How many times have we well-known and confirmed the most incompetent person being appointed to an outfit in which he has no clue of its operations? An example, a doctor of medicine being appointed a director general of mining and exploration or vice versa!

Leaders need advice in what they do and what they fail to do. It is their responsibility to accept or reject advice. The advice to the leaders is a motivation or motivator for their actions in time of decision-making. No leader that we know of, ever went out in the field alone without advisors. Even King Solomon had many advisors with all his wisdom that he had acquired from God on request. Advisors teamed up in King Solomon's courtyards to enjoy his wisdom and judgments.

In our own opinion, all leaders today are "turncoats" or the people who make wavering decisions to be denied and disowned later in their lives. They are simply, "Vigeugeus" who do this thing today and do another thing tomorrow due to the weak human nature of their unpredictable circumstances and the surroundings. Leaders behave circumstantially, they also behave biologically, physically, morally and environmentally. That is, they behave depending on what they do, who they are and at where they are in life at the time of making their wavering decisions which they deny the following day.

However, Ameru People of Kenya are never swayed or wavered by anything because they are a focused people. They always make well-thought, calculated and lasting decisions. They have their own giants in thought, beliefs, principles, views, opinions and tenets which in Kimeru, they pragmatically and prudently refer to as Laing'o CIA Ngai in Meru.

CHAPTER TWO

2.0 FORERUNNERS OF TRIBALISM IN KENYA

The earliest recorded foreign visitor in the East African Coast – Kenya is One Portuguese Vasco da Gama who reached Mombasa via South African Coast in 1498. However, he did not relate well with the natives. He therefore discriminated against those whom he first met in the region and even he called them names. His first impression was that, there were good and bad natives within the environment. After one week he thought it prudent to sail farther to Malindi to find more friendly people with whom he established the first Nguuntune East African base at Gede (today Gede Ruins in Malindi).

Before that, the Coast had been visited by the Arabs who searched and captured Africans who lived in the Coastal Islands and among them were the Ameru community who lived in Manda Island, Kenya. The Ameru had long occupied Manda Island from Egypt around AD 1100. Therefore, Ameru were targets of the Slave Trade by Arabs many centuries even before the arrival of Nguuntune (the Portuguese) who wore red clothes or turbans.

For the Portuguese and others, the Mombasa's natural harbor instantly attracted their foreign attention and therefore a Turkish expedition built a small Fort there in 1589. However, Portuguese fearing for the security of their route back to Portugal, they attacked and took Mombasa from the Turks in 1593, and they began at once to build a large Fort to guard the harbor entrance as their own. The Portuguese (Nguuntune) regarded themselves as the representatives of Christendom rather than that of Portugal and for that reason they sailed under the flag of the "Order of Christ Jesus" and therefore an obvious name of the new Fort that they built in the name of Jesus (Fort Jesus).

When Fort Jesus was built, its angular form was dictated by the rules of military defense by one Italian architect from Goa, Joao Batista Cairato. For record and information, Fort Jesus has suffered a history of murders, sieges, blockades, starvations, bombardments and treachery that makes human modern world of hi-jacking and thuggery seem quite tamed by any standards in comparison.

At the time, Portuguese seemed living in their own land or colony of not more than one hundred strong Portuguese men in their own Kingdom away from home that was separated from home by treacherous six months' sailing back home. The Portuguese enjoyed living at the Kenyan Coast from AD 1500 to AD 1729 when they left Mombasa for good after over a cool two centuries.

Fort Jesus has preserved the same basic shape as when it was built over 400 years ago. Such long and clear visions into the past are rare today and therefore, if you happen to visit and leave Mombasa without visiting that major landmark in the history of East Africa, you may find a cause for regret afterwards in life. It is the only monument that has remained intact, while it has withstood time, ages and lived for over 400 years.

The events in the history of Mombasa are deliberately and purposely recorded here by the writer to connect it with the history of Ameru who lived in Mboa (Manda Island for over four centuries) in Kenya before they were disturbed by the (Nguuntune) Portuguese, when they were hunted down as resilient and spirited laborers to build the walls of Fort Jesus in 1593.

Our point in this connection is to remember that when Fort Jesus was built in Mombasa in 1593, the Ameru people were the builders and laborers at the Fort, having been captured as slaves from Manda Island that was their home at the time. Ameru had been hunted down as slaves by the Arabs since 1100 AD on their arrival from Egypt where they were expert Pyramids (Mbiira/Graves) builders.

To confirm our story, at Gede Ruins, in Malindi today, there are some remnants of the wonders of Ameru expertise in constructions. At the same site, there are buildings and model Courts where the Nguuntune (Portuguese) lived to judge and condemn Ameru to serve prison sentences as a way of extracting labor from the innocent natives. Ameru were the most tolerant and resilient people who were hardworking and capable of providing labor under those severe circumstances. They provided labor under duress and coercion as slaves to construct Fort Jesus.

There is also a very deep dry well at Gede Ruins where the Ameru were required to remove an orange from its bottom without touching it. That was one of the tricks and guiles or craftiness that they were required to perform before they would be allowed to live free and comfortable life in their homes in Manda Island by the Nguuntune (the Portuguese) who had become their first colonizers.

The Nguuntune (the Portuguese) had overwhelmed the Ameru by the power of their powder-guns. Thus, the Ameru felt threatened and disturbed by the Nguuntune who had colonized them. Truly, before the arrival of the British Colonialists, the Ameru people had encountered other colonizers before. That was around AD 1520, before the Portuguese pulled out of Malindi where they had settled up to 1593, during which time, they had identified those hardworking people (Ameru) for their labor to construct the Fort at Mombasa.

Between 12th, and 16th, Centuries the Ameru had lived in Mboa (Manda Island) Kenya, where they were hunted by the Arabs as slaves to many parts of the world. The arrival of the Portuguese (Nguuntune) in 15th, Century only heightened the Slave Trade Market to extend to America. Specifically, history confirms that the Portuguese in 1490's arrived at Mombasa through one Vasco da Gama who was simply an explorer.

The Portuguese had arrived in parties and first settled at Malindi where Vasco da Gama had erected his Pillar in 1498. That Pillar has stood and defied time and ages. By that time, Ameru had already settled in Mboa (Manda Island), more than four centuries before. When the Portuguese arrived in the East African Coast, they found a people (Ameru) who were hardworking and resilient to the hot climate who could perform hard tasks as laborers.

It was at Malindi (today Gede Ruins) where the Portuguese used to detain their slaves after being captured from Mboa (Manda Island) between AD 1500 and AD 1593, when they left Malindi for Mombasa to build Fort Jesus. You can therefore, visualize the damage they had caused to Ameru people in Mboa (Manda Island) through slavery of the people they had hunted and captured for export to America. They had hunted and captured Ameru as slaves for around one century and this is how they used to do it!

It is that, when the Portuguese raided the villages in Mboa, they made the natives believe that they had committed some crimes and therefore, they were being arrested to be judged and be imprisoned somewhere outside Mboa (Manda Island). Then they captured their victims as criminals and forced them out of their villages. When captives left Manda Island, they were kept at Gede Slaves Camp where they went through mock interrogation that confined them to serve a prison sentence in disguise as slaves. The prison sentence was supposed to be served at Fort Jesus where they were utilized as workers to construct and extend the Fort.

Those who had served their sentence while constructing Fort Jesus never went back home, instead they were exported to America as slaves. It was through the lower corridor of the Fort that they went through into the ships that exported them to Americas without others knowing their fate. The Portuguese had traded in slavery using Ameru commodity for nearly a century before they finally left Malindi for Mombasa. At Gede Ruins, in Malindi, visitors to the site have never clearly been told why a "Chain still fastened to the oldest tree" that exists within the compound without being disturbed. To the visitors, the Chain is just a mark of rotten history! Nobody wants to know the cause of its existence at the site.

While people were taken there as slaves in America, they were made to work in the Sugar Plantations in the Caribbean Islands believing that they were still serving their prison sentences, but with some freedom to enjoy their family relationships within the Plantations. That is, they were slaves with some privileges to multiply and increase the number of slaves for their masters. In the Caribbean Islands, you will find Ameru people who became slaves in America from the 16th, century.

When the Nguuntune withdrew from Malindi at Gede Ruins, where they used to keep the Ameru captured from Manda Island, the Ameru had their golden opportunity to plan to escape from Mboa (Manda Island) in order to go to settle elsewhere and indeed they managed to live peaceful lives after leaving Mboa. That is the true account and connection of the story of Ameru with Mombasa where Ameru have continued their trade of Miraa for nearly a century.

We have given a chronicle of how Mombasa was occupied by foreigners, while the inhabitants lived in fear of being captured as slaves for export to America in another book titled "Walking in Kenyan History" in Amazon.com. In Mombasa, the true natives of the coast lived in the remote villages avoiding to be captured as slaves, and therefore, they visited the town as if they were visitors from the periphery. It is only recently that Coastal People, started to approach Mombasa as their own City and without fear because they feared the foreigners in their past. If the Arabs never safeguarded the Kenyan Coast, the Nguuntune (the Portuguese) would have remained there until the Kenya's Independence Day, since other communities had no power to wrestle with Nguuntune. The Arabs fought fierce wars with the Portuguese to protect the Kenyan Coast. Though, they also involved themselves with Slavery from the time immemorial when they populated the Oceanic Islands of Samoa, Tonga, Vanuatu, Kiribati, Nauru, Tuvalu, Fiji and others Islands in the Pacific Ocean.

CHAPTER THREE

3.0 HOW COLONIALISTS CREATED KENYAN TRIBES

When the Europeans arrived in Kenya from 1840's to 1880's they found all tribes of Kenya already settled in their respective settlements as the original inhabitants of those habitations. The only people who had not fully settled by 1880's were the Turkana people who were still in their emigrational journey onward from Nandi and Baringo Communities which pushed them farther northwards.

Elsewhere in Kenya, the arrival of the colonizers found a people who were already settled and organized in their different communities within Kenya. The only thing that the colonizers did was to negotiate and draw the boundaries and borders between the communities whom they named tribes for their own interests and ease of administration and governance. Remember at this point, it were the Europeans who named and divided Kenyans as tribes. Kenyans had no word as "Tribe" in any language which in Kiswahili was translated to "Kabila." That Kabila in Kiswahili has never found a "proper-word" meaning in any language in Kenya; nearer to it is, "Wameru, Wakamba, Waembu, Wajaluo, Waluyhia, Wakalenjin, Wataita, Waswahili, Wamaasai, Wakikuyu, Wagiriama and others.

Word "Wa" did not mean tribe, it meant people who lived in those places. But the colonizers called them tribe or kabila for their own convenience.

In Kenya, before the colonizers' arrival, communities used to call themselves by the name of their residential places, like Wameru (the people who lived in Meru, Nandi, Kipsigis, Kisumu, Siaya, Murang'a, Nyeri, Kitui, Machakos, Mandera, Wajir, Taita, Kwale, Kajiado, Narok, Kisii, Kakamega, Nakuru, Embu and Laikipia and so on). People belonged to their areas of resident and not tribes. They were Wameru of Meru and not tribe of Ameru. Tribe is a creation of the Europeans for their convenience in governance.

When the Colonizers arrived in Kenya, the Arabs, Portuguese and Turkish traders had traded in the coastal towns exchanging African slaves and ivory as their ready commodities in the past centuries. The major towns in the Kenyan coast in AD 1400's were by then, Mombasa, Gede, Malindi and Lamu. The

Coastal Towns of Kenya were principally inhabited by the Arabs who hunted the locals as slaves for export to the Pacific Islands already mentioned above. The Wataita, Wataveta and Mijikenda were living in the peripheries of those towns where the Arabs never wanted them to know that they were slave traders. However, when Arabs captured Ameru from Manda Island for export to the Pacific Islands, they found some girls suitable for marriage and they married them as wives. Arabs never wanted to intermingle with locals in marriage directly, but instead they selected some beautiful slave-girls from Manda Island and married them. The following paragraph has been quoted from "Encarta Premium" writers as a proof that Waswahili were products of Africans (specifically Ameru people when they lived in Manda Island between AD 1000 and AD 1480's) before the arrival of Europeans in AD 1498.

3.1 WASWAHILI WERE NEW PRODUCTS IN KENYA

The trans-Saharan slave trade grew significantly from the 10th to the 15th century, as vast African empires such as Ghana, Mali, Songhai, and Kanem-

Bornu developed south of the Sahara and marshaled the trade. Arab slave raiders also penetrated south, up the Nile River to the present-day Ethiopia, capturing thousands of slaves and sending them down the Nile to Egypt.

Over the course of more than a thousand years, the trans-Saharan slave trade saw the movement of at least 10 million enslaved men, women, and children from West and East Africa to North Africa, the Middle East and India. The slaves and their descendants contributed to the harems, royal households and armies of the Arab, Turkish and Persian rulers in those regions.

Also, by the 9th century, seafaring Muslims from Arabia and Persia had made their way down the Indian Ocean, Coast of East Africa obtaining African slaves in ports from Mogadishu (in present-day Somalia) to Sofala (in present-day Mozambique) and conveying them to western Asian cities to work as slaves.

"The culture of the East African Coastal regions was strongly influenced by Arab and Persian traders many of whom intermarried with Africans (specifically Ameru who lived in Manda Island, and these are our own words in history search and making) thus producing the Swahili people and their culture."

Those Swahili people spread along the East African Coast very fast from Manda Island to Mtwara in Tanzania. Between the 9th and the 13th centuries, this Arab-Persian-Swahili population established cities and city-states along the East African Coast. These cities and states captured or purchased slaves from the East African interior for domestic and agricultural tasks. In the 18th and 19th centuries, as plantation agriculture developed in the region, the East African slave trade increased dramatically.

Scholars' opinions however, differ on the issue of the long-term effects of Islam on African slavery. Some believe that Islamic law helped regulate slavery, thus limiting its abuses; these scholars often argue that because Islam encouraged the freeing of slaves upon their master's death, it also increased instances of emancipation. Other scholars believe that Islam led to the expansion of slavery, arguing that at the time that slavery was growing in the parts of Africa coming under Islamic influence, slavery was declining in most of medieval Europe." What is important to note is that Arabs were the first slave traders in Africa and not the Portuguese (the Nguuntune) as people are made to believe.

Arabs exported Africans to North Africa, Middle East, India and in the Pacific Ocean Islands of Tonga, Samoa, Tuvalu, Nauru, Vanuatu, Kiribati, Fiji, Niue, Palau and others early in those centuries. All the names of those Islands are Bantu by pronunciation and deep in their meanings. People have never bothered to find out why all those group of Islands bear Bantu names. The languages spoken in those Islands are also very similar and close to Bantu languages in Africa.

The intermarriage of Arabs with Africans (Ameru women slaves who attracted Arabs men became wives) produced a people whom they named "Waswahili" (people of the mixed races) who spoke a neat interspersing of Kimeru and Arabic words that produced a new language known as Kiswahili (corrupted Kimeru language) as indicated below. Since Waswahili (people of the mixed races) were the products of Arabs and Ameru people, the Kimeru words when compared to Kiswahili words, do match

96% similar. One fact is that Ameru people were in existence with their Kimeru language before they intermarried with Arabs to produce the people (of the mixed people) whom they named Waswahili at the Coast with their new language (Kiswahili). Swahili simply means a "mix of people and languages."

Funny enough, that new language of Arabs and Ameru which came into existence around AD 1200 became an important Bantu language to be easily understood by many people in East Africa though it was spoken by a minority people who were accredited and acknowledged travelers. People from Arabia were travelers since time immemorial. You will remember people like Ibn Battuta, the great traveler.

Through the travelers, the language spread throughout East Africa very fast and quickly. Since its speakers were travelers in East Africa, the language was adopted by those who came into contact with them. The language became popular among the Coastal people of East Africa and it spread to the hinterland where people their spoke mother tongue plus Kiswahili as a middle language for the traders.

3.2 WASWAHILI ARE PRODUCTS OF AMERU

Look at the following words in Kiswahili and Kimeru languages which are 96% similar in pronunciation and spelling. Where they differ it is only by a small margin in spelling but not in pronunciation. Throughout in history of languages and their similarities, Kimeru and Kiswahili languages are the same language. Ameru and Waswahili in Kenya live far apart from each other and yet they speak a language that has 96% similar words.

When Ameru were captured as slaves who were exported to the Oceanic Islands by the Arabs before the arrival of the Europeans in AD 1500, Arabs had found beautiful wives among their slaves with whom they married to produce a people who spoke a mixed language known as Kiswahili, while the new people were known as Waswahili.

KITHOHIRI, in Kimeru means "you have mixed me up" and therefore when the new products came to be a people who had been mixed up through the intermarriage of Arabs and Ameru, they adopted their name Kiswahili as they could pronounce the word.

Compare the following words in Kimeru and the new language that came to be before the arrival of the Europeans in East African Coast from AD 1498.

No.	English name	Kiswahili name (new)	Kimeru name (old)
1	House	Nyumba	Nyumba
2	Cow	Ng'ombe	Ng'ombe
3	Cat	Paka	Mpaka
4	Goat	Mbuzi	Mburi
5	Water	Maji	Ruuji
6	Food	Chakula	Biakuria
7	Clothes	Nguo	Nguo
8	Person	Mtu	Muntu
8	Persons	Watu	Antu
9	People	Watu	Antu
10	Race	Kabila	Kabira
11	Breast	Kivua	Kivara
12	Head	Kichwa	Mutwe
13	Leg	Mguu	Kuguru

13	Knee	Magoti	Maru
14	Finger	Kidole	Kiara
15	Door	Mlango	Murango
16	Visitor	Mgeni	Mugeni
17	Thief	Mwizi	Mwamba
18	Shoes	Viatu	Iratu
18	Patch	Kiraka	Kiraka
19	Woman	Mwanamke	Muka
20	Youngman	Kijana	Kaana
21	Fingers	Vidole	Biara
22	A day	Siku	Ntuku
23	Charcoal	Makaa	Makara
24	Porridge	Uji	Uchuru
25	Lie	Uongo	Urongo
25	Liar	Muongo	Murongo
26	Truth	Ukweli	Ukweri
27	Prayers	Maombi	Maromba
28	World	Nchi	Nthiguru
29	Cloth	Kitambaa	Gitambaa
30	Money	Pesha	Mbecha
30	Currency	Noti	Noti
31	Motorcar	Gari	Ngari
32	Owner	Mwenyewe	Mwene
33	Church	Kanisa	Kanisa

34	Cup	Kikombe	Kikombe
34	Cup	Kibaba	Kibaba
34	Cupboard	Kavati	Kabati
35	Banana	Mgomba	Mukomba
36	Potatoes	Viazi	Ikwachii
37	Firewoods	Kuni	Nkuu
37	Fire	Moto	Mwanki
38	Play	Mchezo	Muchetho
39	To sing	Kuimba	Kwina
40	To sell	Kuuza	Kwendia
41	To borrow	Kuomba	Kuromba
42	To pay	Kulipa	Kuria
43	Increase	Kuongeza	Kuongera
44	To drink	Kunyua	Kunyua
45	Cultivate	Kulima	Kurima
46	To eat	Kula	Kuria
47	Millet	Mawele	Mwere
48	Oranges	Machungwa	Machungwa
49	Lemons	Ndimu	Ndimu
50	School	Shule	Sukuru
51	Important	Maana	Maana
52	Wound	Kindonda	Kironda
53	Bag	Chondo	Kiondo
53	Bag	Ngunia	Ngunia

54	Back	Mgongo	Mwongo
55	Tin	Debe	Ndebe
56	Pail/bucket	Mtungi	Mutungi
57	Cabbages	Mboga	Mpoka
58	Meat	Nyama	Nyama
59	Hen	Kuku	Nguku
60	Sufuria	Sufuria	Suburia
61	Stove	Jiko	Riiko
62	Chair	Kiti	Giti
63	Table	Meza	Metha
64	Plate	Saani	Thaani
65	Spoon	Kijiko	Gichiko
66	Sand	Mchanga	Muthanga
67	Blanket *	Mrengeti	Muringiti
68	Mat	Mkeka	Mweka
69	Basket	Kikavu	Ikabu
70	Stones	Mawe	Maiga
71	Road	Njia	Njira
72	Oil/fat	Mafuta	Mauta
73	Songs	Nyimbo	Ndwimbo
74	Camel	Ngamia	Nkamiira
75	Panga	Panga	Kibanga
76	Shop *	Duka	Nduka
77	Bridge	Daraja	Ndaraca

78	Pocket	Mvuko	Mubuko
79	Mole	Huko	Mpuko
80	Knife	Kishu	Kichiu
81	Skin	Ngozi	Ngoci
82	Sheep	Kondoo	Ng'ondu
83	Donkey	Punda	Bunda
84	Hill	Mlima	Kirima
85	River	Mto	Mwera
86	Well	Kisima	Kithima
87	Arrowroot	Nduma	Ituma
88	Banana	Ndizi	Ndigu
89	Sheet	Shuka	Chuka
90	Cry	Lia	Kurira
91	Sisal	Makonge	Makonge
92	Driver*	Dereva	Ndereba
93	Government*	Serikali	Thirikari
94	King	Mfalme	Mugwe
95	Court	Mahakama	Njuri
96	Party *	Chama	Kiama
97	Years	Miaka	Miaka
98	Age	Umri	Ukuru
99	Riches	Utajiri	Utonga
100	Agriculture	Kilimo	Urimi
101	Hyena	Fisi	Mbiti

102	Lightning	Radhi	Rweni
103	Onions	Kitunguu	Gitunguru
104	Eggs	Mayai	Mayai
105	Footsteps	Nyayo	Makinyo
106	Clouds	Mawingu	Matu
107	Sun	Jua	Riua
108	Stars	Nyota	Njota
109	Moon	Mwezi	Mweri
110	Soil	Mchanga	Muthetu
111	Tree	Mti	Muti
112	Roots	Misisi	Miri
113	Witchcraft	Urogi/Uchawi	Urogi
114	Saliva	Mate	Mata
115	Tongue	Ulimi	Rurimi
116	Eyes	Macho	Meetho
117	Guineafoul	Kanga	Nkanga
118	Pig	Ngurwe	Ngurwe
119	Leaves	Mayani	Mayani
120	Razor blade *	Wembe	Rwembe
121	Jembe	Jembe	Icembe
122	Bow	Uta	Uta
123	Arrows	Michale	Migwi
124	Greengrams	Ndengu	Ndengu
125	Matchbox	Kiberiti	Kibiriti

126	Pen	Kalamu	Karamu
127	Ash	Jibu	Muju
128	Waist	Kiuno	Kiuno
129	Neck	Shingo	Nkingo
130	Imprisonment *	Kivungo	Kibungo
130	Prison *	Jela	Nchera
131	Hand	Mkono	Mukono
132	Night	Usiku	Utuku
133	Teeth	Meeno	Maiyo
134	Dirt	Usafu	Ruko
135	Cleanliness	Usafi	Utheru
136	Mouth	Mdomo	Muromo
137	Pipe *	Mfereji	Muberethi
138	Boundaries	Mipaka	Mianka
139	Bread	Mkate	Mugate
140	Education	Masomo	Kithomo
141	Bell	Kengele	Nkengere
142	Life	Maisha	Maicha
143	Journey	Safari	Chabari
143	Love	Upendo	Rwendo
144	Evil	Ubaya	Uthuku
145	Two	Mbili	Ijili
146	Three	Tatu	Ithatu

147	Four	Nne	Inya
148	Five	Tano	Ithano
149	Nine	Kenda/Tisa	Kenda
150	Ten	Kumi	Ikumi
151	Ladle	Mwiko	Mwiko
152	Ants	Mswa	Muthoa
153	Salary *	Msahara	Muchara
154	Father	Baba	Baaba
155	Mother	Mama	Maama
156	Valley	Mteremko	Muteremuko
157	God	Mungu	Murungu
158	Yam	Kikwa	Gikwa
159	Name	Jina	Riitwa
160	Before	Mbele	Mbere
161	Ribs	Mbafu	Mbaru
162	Mat	Mkeka	Mweka
163	Foods	Vyakula	Biakuria
164	Hair	Nywele	Njuiri
165	Length	Ureefu	Uraaja
165	Sugarcane	Miwa	Kiwa
166	Many	Nyingi	Inyingi
167	Fruits	Matunda	Matunda
168	Snake	Nyoka	Njoka
169	Horse*	Farasi	Mbarathi

170	To plan	Kupanga	Kubanga
171	Scar	Kilema	Kilema
172	Debt	Deni	Irandu
173	Toilet	Choo	Kioro
174	Elephant	Ndovu	Njogu
175	Fly	Nzi	Ngi
176	Mutilate	Kuketa	Kutana
177	Collect	Kuokota	Kurogota
178	Sweater *	Fulana	Burana
179	Angel	Malaika	Mulaika
180	Grave	Kaburi	Kaburi
181	Laziness	Uvivu	Uthao
182	Hammer *	Nyundo	Nyondo
183	Craftiness	Ukora	Ukora
184	Foolishness	Ujinga	Uchinka
185	Bones	Mifupa	Miruitu
186	Paper	Karatasi	Karataci
187	Additional	Nyongezi	Mpongeri
188	Hat	Kofia	Nkobia
189	Roots	Misisi	Miri
190	Buttons	Vifungo	Ibungo
191	Comb	Kisanuo	Gichanuri
192	Oldman	Mzee	Muthee
193	Bamboo tree	Mrangi	Murangi

194	Rope	Mkanda	Mukanda
195	Needle	Sindano	Chindano
196	Gold	Dhaabu	Thaabu
197	Witness	Mzaidi	Mathoiri
198	Locust	Nzige	Ngige
199	Saltlick	Mwonyo	Mwonyo
200	Case *	Kesi	Igamba
201	Bottle*	Supa	Suba
202	Face	Usho	Uthiu
203	Beer*	Pombe	Nchoobi
204	Epilepsy	Kifafa	Kibaba
205	Trade	Biashara	Biashara
206	Craftsman	Fundi	Bundi
207	Tea	Chai	Chai
208	Let's go	Twende	Twite
209	Die	Kufa	Kua
210	Cut	Kata	Giita
211	Get lost	Toroka	Gutoroka
212	To hide	Kufisa	Kuitha
213	To break	Kuvunjika	Kunika
214	To roar	Kuguruma	Kuruuma
215	To draw	Kuchota	Gutaa
216	To steal	Kwuiva	Kwiija
217	To sleep	Kulala	Kumama

218	To love	Kwenda	Kupenda
219	To refuse	Kukataa	Kurega
220	To receive	Kupokea	Kubokera
221	To inform	Kwarifu	Kwiira
222	To slaughter	Kuchinja	Kuthinja
223	To forgive	Kuchamea	Guchamira
224	To draw water	Chota maji	Gutaa ruuji
225	To protest	Kubishana	Kubisana
226	To escape	Kutoroka	Gutoroka
227	To graze	Kulisha	Kurithia
228	To beseech	Kubembeleza	Kwerenca
229	To plant	Kupanda	Kuanda
230	To cultivate	Kulima	Kurima
231	To borrow	Kukopa	Gukoba
232	To greet	Kusalimia	Gukethania
233	To soothe	Kuboresha	Kuboreria
234	Be happy	Kufurai	Kugwirua
235	Be unhappy	Kukashirika	Kuthuura
236	To cook	Kupika	Kuruga
237	Add	Kuongeza	Kuongera
238	Beat	Kupiga	Kuringa
239	Sit down	Kaa chini	Kara nthi
240	To buy	Kununua	Kugura
241	To crush	Kukanyanga	Gukinyanga

242	Steel	Chuma	Chuma
243	Ears	Masikio	Matu
244	Stairs	Ngazi	Nkathi
245	Luck	Bahati	Baati
246	To wash	Kusafisa	Kuthambia
247	Mud	Matope	Mutolo
248	To fry	Kukaanga	Gukaranga
249	To carry	Kubeba	Gukamata
250	To rot	Kuosha	Kuora
251	To ripe	Kuiva	Kuirua
252	To play	Kuchecha	Kuthaka
253	To stay	Kukaa	Gukara
254	To slaughter	Kunyonga	Kunyonga
255	To point at	Kuelekeza	Kuerekeria
256	You arrange	Mtapanga	Bukabanga
257	You will get	Mtapata	Bukagwata
258	You will cry	Utalia	Ukarira
259	You swallow	Utameza	Ukameria
260	You will learn	Utazoma	Ukathoma
261	Intestines	Matumbo	Matumbo
262	Drought	Ukame	Ukame

3.3 A NEW THEORY OF AMERU AND WASWAHILI

WE PROPOSE A NEW THEORY: KISWAHILI LANGUAGE AS THE LINGUA FRANCA OF EAST AFRICA IS MORE CLOSER TO KIMERU LANGUAGE IN THE WHOLE OF EAST AFRICA

Our portent and augury question is, who borrowed similar words from the other? Who copied words from the other? Who imitated the other? Who existed before the other? Who taught the other their language? Why only these two (Ameru and Waswahili) communities have utmost similar words in their languages?

Look at Number 200, where the Mswahili had not learnt about cases in court (during the pre-colonization era) and after they had been left on his own, where they had no better word of their own for the new word "case" which in Kimeru is Igamba. When Mmeru was introduced to Courts many years after parting with the Waswahili, Mmeru had the word for the case, while the Mswahili had no word for the case! Mswahili was short of his new words without the support of Mmeru (the parents') words. Even today Mswahili calls case, "Kesi yako" while Mmeru has the word dissimilar to that of Mswahili.

Take the word Kengele, (bell in English) and Nkengere in Kimeru, the words are very similar in pronunciation and spelling. It is not a coincidence but a chance in happening. The bell (Nkengere) existed among the Ameru in Mboa approximately in AD 1100 when they arrived there, and that is how the Waswahili the product of intermarriage (of Arabs and Africans even if not Ameru) came up with a name Kengele, a name similar to that of Ameru. Therefore, the new theory is, "Either that Ameru sometimes lived with the Waswahili or they interacted with them from some beginning in their lives."

Our theory therefore is that, "Since it is only parents who are capable of teaching their language to their children, Ameru and Waswahili must have lived together in their past and one of them must have lived and existed as the parent and the other as a child to have a close or similar language."

That is not a complicated theory to accept and embrace while linguists continue to investigate for confirmation. We believe that Ameru were the parents of Waswahili because Ameru intermarried with the Arabs to produce a people known as Waswahili (mixed people and languages) in an era before the arrival of the Europeans in East Coast of Africa in AD 1498 when one Vasco da Gama who we learn in history built his Pillar in Malindi. The Pillar that has defied time and ages.

For sure the Waswahili lived along the 10 Mile Coastal Strip that was controlled by the Arabs from long ago and that was before the Portuguese had arrived in East Africa. Therefore, Waswahili must have come to be existent when the Arabs intermingled with Ameru on capturing them as slaves, although that was between AD 1000 and AD 1480's before the arrival of the Europeans in East Africa. The truth is that, Waswahili lived in the Arab towns along the coast from Vanga to Lamu and Manda Island to Kiunga while Ameru lived in Manda Island between the same period and therefore, the Waswahili spoke a language similar to Ameru because they lived together as their descendants and progenies.

The truth is that, in Kenya there is no other community whose words are more similar to Kiswahili than Kimeru whose words were slanted by the (new breed of a people whom they named Waswahili) people who were the offspring of Arabs and Ameru who intermarried between AD 1000 and 1480's. That had happened before the arrival of the Europeans who later became the enemy of the people who had practiced slavery along the Coast of East Africa and also in the West African Coast. Euopeans came to Africa uniquely to stamp out slavery in the World and then to colonize the people whom they had freed from slavery. The last States to abolish Slavery in America were in 1833 and 1848, despite the fact that Slavery had been abolished in 1807.

It is interesting how Kiswahili (a new language) became the "Lingua Franca of East Africa" yet it was spoken by a minority people in the region. But the fact is that it was easily understood by the Arabs who also spread it among the people they came into contact with in their travels in East Africa. The "new language" also became the favorite among the people of Kenya including those who spoke their own languages.

Coastal people easily picked many words of Kiswahili and mixed them into their languages as if Kiswahili was their mother-tongue. Sooner or later, many communities in East Africa adopted Kiswahili as their "mother tongue" while it became the "Lingua Franca of East Africa." It is said that, Kiswahili language is a gift language from God for East Africans who speak the language from childhoods without a teacher. That at birth, a child can pick a Kiswahili word without a teacher naturally. The question is, "Why?"

However, Kenyans have never bothered to dig deep into that interesting history of the Kenyan Coastal People prior to 1840's when the Missionaries like Dr. Ludwig Krapf and John Rebmann who were not colonizers arrived in Mombasa, Kenya. The actual missionaries arrived in Kenya not to colonize but to spread the Gospel of Christ to the people and so that Enslavers would stop enslaving others through the Gospel of Christ. That is, if the colonizers never arrived in Kenya, tribes would not have been formed or occurred in Kenya because communities would have lived without knowing what tribalism meant in their lives.

There is a stimulating and inspiring history of the Kenyan Coast, when Africans were hunted and captured as slaves by the Portuguese (between AD 1500 and AD 1870's). The captives were driven through the Legendary Corridor of Fort Jesus, Mombasa which was built in 1593 using Ameru as the laborers. Therefore, from 1593 or even earlier up to 1870'S, there is a period of more than three and half centuries (370 years), an Era that is unaccounted for in the history of Kenya. Communities should be encouraged to investigate and reveal their past histories.

Coastal people, the Mijikenda, Wataita and Wataveta, Wakamba or Wa Pokomo and Oromo have never accounted for their existence during that Epoch. Their history and activities have never revealed where they were and what they did in that Epoch of their history. Their history remains blank, we only capture them during colonization and while they only narrate how and when the Europeans arrived in their midst.

That is because nobody inscribed anything about it leading to what is called the "Blank History of the Kenyan Coast" which urgently needs revisiting in future. We beg the revisiting of that history of the coast from time immemorial to AD 1498 when Vasco da Gama visited Mombasa. We are talking about the "unmitigated history" from AD 1000 to AD 1480's before the arrival of the Portuguese in the name of one Vasco da Gama in 1498. That is the era in which Arabs had mingled and intermarried with Africans to produce a new community known as Waswahili in Kenya.

The era of the "Blank history of the Coast" from AD 1000 to AD 1480's is the period when Ameru intermarried with the Arabs as they chose among them "fair ladies" for marriage in order to produce the new people whom they named "Waswahili" which also in Arabic meant "new people or new community." That new people's language became their favorite language which spread far and wide among the people in East Africa.

The "Epoch of Kenyan Coast Blank History" has fully never been revealed or explained by any historian, be it by ordinary or extraordinary authority. That Epoch has remained a mystery to the Kenyans who would want to understand what happened in Kenya between AD 1000 and AD 1498 when the first

Portuguese arrived in Mombasa as an explorer. Still, there is an Epoch in the history of Kenya that has never been studied by historians to reveal what Kenyans were doing between AD 1500's and AD 1880's when the first Europeans arrived as colonizers. Communities in Kenya never emphasize that Epoch in history because they never want to accept their past and the fact that they were hunted by Arabs for export as slaves to the Oceanic Islands before AD 1490's.

As for Ameru History, the "Epoch of the Kenyan Coast Blank History" is covered in how they lived and progressed in their life in Manda Island and beyond, after they had undertaken an epic journey from Egypt through the wilderness of Nubia Desert and Congo Forests, through Rwanda, Tanzania Serengeti and Mtito Andei in Kenya to Manda Island in Kenya. Ameru community believe that they have been sojourners through various Epochs of life since time immemorial.

Ameru community is jam-packed with Epochs in history from creation in the Middle East to crossing the Red Sea, from their life in Egypt to their escape from Egypt, from arriving and living in Manda Island to their escape from Manda Island, from their heroic trek from Manda Island to their arrival and settlement in Merulands. Ameru have a long history to tell and narrate to other communities.

CHAPTER FOUR

4.0 CHALLENGE TO THE HISTORIANS IN KENYA

4.1 WHERE DID ARABS EXPORT THEIR SLAVES TO?

We need to know where Arabs exported their slaves whom they captured from East Africa before AD 1500's. This is because slavery existed even before AD 1498 at the arrival of the first Portuguese in East Africa who was named Vasco da Gama. By positive imagination, we also know and believe that slaves were exported to the Pacific Islands by the Arabs who dealt in slavery many centuries earlier since slavery existed centuries before. Arabs had exported their slaves in North Africa, Middle East, India and beyond many centuries before AD 1500's after which the Europeans entered the Slave Trade.

When the Europeans entered the Slave Trade to export their commodity to Americas, every community in Kenya seems to have lived in darkness as nobody talks about their community during that "Epoch of Communities' Silence." That "Epoch of Communities' Silence" in Kenya is for many communities other than Ameru who forever do account and associate the Epoch as their life in Mboa (Manda Island) Kenya, before they were disturbed by the Portuguese (Nguuntune) who hunted them as slaves from 1500's. Ameru have always accounted for their Epochs since the time they left Egypt where they had lived as Pyramids (Mbiira corruption of words) builders.

The other Epoch that many communities in Kenya never account for, is the period between the Portuguese arrival in Kenya in AD 1498 and the time of Colonization in 1880's. Many communities in Kenya have never revealed what they were doing during that Epoch because most communities treat that Epoch as non-existence in their lives. Kenyans would want to know from each community what they did and what they did not do during that Epoch and other Epochs in their history.

However, the making of the actual and authentic Kenyan history for all the communities began in 1884, when Carl Peters, a 24-year-old smart

German historian, carried a hammock and crisscrossed East Africa armed with a revolver and fiercely forcing many African chiefs to append their "signatures" into some papers that he eventually carried back to Berlin, Germany, claiming that those respective chiefs had ceded their territories to Germany, when Germany was still reluctant to take any colonies at the time.

Meanwhile, William Mackinnon's Imperial British East Africa venture had been supported by the British Foreign Office because it had laid grand schemes to build a "Cape to Cairo Empire." However, in Germany, the leaders quickly realized that Peters wanted to force their country into trouble with other powers through his intentional forgeries. They were intentional because he had his personal motives for signatures.

However, early in February 1885, the German (Reich), Parliament and Kaiser Wilhelm I recognized the known 140,000 square kilometers called Deutsch-Ostafrica (German East Africa), because German Chancellor Otto Bismarck had knowledge that Carl Peters' claims were fraudulent.

As a result, in October 1885, the Berlin Conference (The Scramble for Africa Conference) was called to divide Africa among the separate colonial powers who had already laid their claims to the Continent. Although the British founded the East African Protectorate that year, the Conference had already set rules to be followed on how to make their claims.

Thus, the actual history of Kenya's boundaries started in October 1886, when German Chancellor Otto von Bismarck sent a senior official of his Foreign Affairs Ministry Dr. Friendrich Krauel to London to discuss on the future of a German Protectorate in East Africa.

The discussion between Dr. Friendrich Krauel of Germany and Sir Percy Anderson of UK shaped the future borders of Kenya with its neighbors. Bismark wanted to agree on what was his and what belonged to the British and the Sultan of Zanzibar in East Africa because what Carl Peters seemed to have acquired did not make any sense on the ground. Carl Peters had presented several treaties from East Africa and wanted them signed through Imperial Charter and approved by Parliament in Germany possibly for his own interests.

Bismark had already approved his claim on Tanzania, but he was not clear about the borders for the British East Africa (Kenya and Uganda), though he wanted to expand towards Congo. The Sultan had his issues although the Berlin Conference had already agreed that Sultan's claims were restricted to his claim of 10 Mile Coastal Strip running from the mouth of Tana River in Kenya to the Delta of Ruvuma River in Tanzania.

When the coastal boundaries were settled, London initiated talks on the border between British East Africa and German East Africa from Lake Victoria. In January 1886, Carl Peters and British traders William MacKinnon a Scottish Shipping magnate and Sir Donald Currie discussed the fate of Mt. Kilimanjaro, of which Carl Peters had already informed Berlin it belonged to German, although the Sultan of Zanzibar considered Kilimanjaro part of his territory alongside the 10 Mile Coastal Strip.

In that meeting, Peters wanted the Britons to invest in his company (his interests) and therefore help him take Kilimanjaro, but MacKinnon was also pursuing a Royal Charter for his own company to administer East Africa. Unknown to Peters, Bismark had his own interest in Kilimanjaro as a "lucrative enterprise than any other acquisition." Therefore, the British insisted that if Germans were to keep Kilimanjaro, they were to give other concessions in lieu.

Then Mombasa was put on the table as the "quid pro quo" since it was a gateway to Nyanza, which was strategic as the Victoria was the source of the River Nile. Then quickly, the Germans agreed and swapped Mombasa for their total control of Kilimanjaro. While the ports were under the Sultan, the British were allowed to lease them for their use. Then, Sultan also abandoned his claim over Kilimanjaro as part of German East Africa (Tanganyika).

For some years Kilimanjaro was on the side of Kenya until Queen Victoria gave it to her grandson, Kaiser Wilhelm II of Germany as a birthday present. The 769km line was to pass through Kilimanjaro to the southern tip of Lake Jape which was divided into almost two equal portions to allow both sides have access to it, including Lake Chala being divided into two portions.

Kenya had half of Lake Natron though it dried up later. British were satisfied when German agreed not to make any further concessions on the British side while they were happy to keep the source of the Nile to itself and because they wanted to secure Egypt where construction of the Suez Canal was underway being the gateway that was to change the sea trade forever. In 1890, there was an Anglo-German Commission that changed the boundary between Indian Ocean to the east of Kilimanjaro and it was a change from Ras Jimbo.

Between 1902 and 1906, another Anglo-German commission was carried out when British and German signed a final agreement on 18th, July 1906 establishing the Kenya-Tanzania boundary that exists today. In 1920, Kenya became a colony and the Coastal Strip part that was held on behalf of the Sultan remained as Protectorate of Kenya.

Remember, Britain had leased the Sultan territory on the Kenyan coast at an annuity of £16,000 and that 10 Mile Coastal Strip was ceded by Sultan to Kenya at Independence in 1963. That gave Kenya a coastline which it did not have at the time. Kenya-Uganda boundary had its history between Uganda

Protectorate and British East Africa Protectorate that constructed the Railway to Uganda as a concession of some kind. The Kenya-Ethiopia boundary was agreed in 1907 after Captain Maud had traversed the British territories and Ethiopia in 1902 to come up with "The Maud Line" as the official border between Kenya and Ethiopia after 1907 agreement.

Much later, in 1946 the British suggested to Ethiopian government on the need of boundary changes, which Ethiopia rejected as "The Clifford Line," but after independence, Emperor Haile Selassie and Jomo Kenyatta used their friendship to settle the boundary question with a demarcation of several segments of whose agreement was signed on 15th, November 1963 while the treaty followed and was signed on 9th, June 1970.

Kenya-Sudan border was the most problematic because the key question was the determination of the Turkana grazing grounds and Sudan's access to Lake Turkana through the "Ilemi Triangle" and because British was still unwilling to invest in troops north of Lake Turkana after Ethiopians armed the Nyangatom and Dassanech people with guns after the First World War. Later known as Ngorokos in 1970's!

Much later, Sudan would cede the Ilemi Triangle to Kenya after the agreement of 1907, and when South Sudan started a claim for its independence from Northern Sudan in 1983, Kenya was in the forefront and strong support for South Sudan independence which it gained on 9th, July 2009. All the agreements and treaties for South Sudan were negotiated and signed in Kenya while Sudan became a friend of Kenya from that time, to the extent that Kenyans needed no passport to cross into South Sudan by 2020.

That is how the borders and boundaries of Kenya were secured and protected until what was the Colony and Protectorate of Kenya became Independent and a Republic in December 1963 and December 1964 respectively.

CHAPTER FIVE

5.0 CREATION OF KENYAN TRIBES

Kenya at the time of colonization had 42 tribes according to available colonialists' administration records. Much later in 1993, during Moi Era, five more Districts were created ostensibly to bring government services closer to the people. The new Districts were created out of the old Districts as follows: Migori from Homa Bay, Vihiga from Kakamega, Bomet from Kericho, Makueni from Machakos and Tharaka Nithi from Meru.

The colonizers also had grouped Kenyans into three ethnic groups as Nilos, Bantus and Cushites as a further measure to divide Kenyans for their convenience of colonization. In order to secure and guarantee their governance, the colonizers appointed colonial administrators for each tribe and where tribes occupied vast areas, they appointed several administrators for the tribes, which they named "Districts or Wilaya in Kiswahili."

The Districts were administered by colonial District Commissioners while the eight Provinces were administered by Provincial Commissioners with their respective Headquarters at Nairobi (Nairobi Extra), Garissa (North Eastern), Embu (Eastern), Nyeri (Central), Mombasa (Coast), Nakuru (Rift Valley), Kakamega (Western) and Kisumu (Nyanza).

5.1 JOMO KENYATTA FIRST CABINET

Long ago, there were innocent and clean politicians who lived a "giraffe's life" in Kenya, because giraffes never compete with ordinary animals browsing for the grass on the grounds and therefore they feed at higher levels and at ease. Politicians, nowadays are the real ravenous and gluttonous wolves in conformists' clothing. They feed on rubbish and guile on the grounds from where they are supposed to serve their voters dedicatedly for empowering them to serve their communities without discrimination.

Jomo Kenyatta had his first Cabinet of 18 clean men, three each from Central, Nyanza, Rift Valley and Eastern and one each from Western, Coast and Kisii. Those men were outstanding men of honor who could be trusted by Kenyans in every corner of the country. They administered their allotted and assigned Ministries with vigour, focus, diligence, effort, conscientiousness and attentiveness. Their names were identical with their Ministries as if they were born with those Ministries in their hands, hearts and souls.

Those "18 clean men" were very positive in their lives that they would be ashamed of picking one's needle or stealing someone's one hundred shillings including that of their good employer! Today, politicians have become thieves of public funds and grabbers of personal property in their villages where they are always in courts for this and that misdemeanor. Only God knows the truth about politicians! Few of them are however, honest men and women who carry their names high in public esteem!

Here below, we give the names of the past generations, present and future for young generations to note, learn and maintain so that they will not complain that they did not know their age groups and age sets. The example in the table applies to all tribes of Kenya that circumcise their men.

As for those whose minds are inquisitive, will ask, "Where did you get that information?" The answer is, the information has been there, but it is diminishing every day for lack of activation. For example, if you have a book in your home bookshelf and you never open its pages for about twenty years, the book will gather dust and in the end it will be of no use, when finally, it will be deleted (forgotten) from the records.

This is why we have searched the past records to ensure that some of our customs are activated. You are therefore, invited to read the CHRONICLE to find the date of your great grandfather, your grandfather, your father and your age group including that of your son because Ameru History is open and alive in progress for the generations to come.

Remember, the age groups cut across and spread all over Kenya because almost every tribe in Kenya do circumcise their sons as a matter of customs, culture and traditions. Thus, every tribe in Kenya can use the same table to match their age groups in their respective communities for the purpose of comparison and future Kenyan Census Exercise.

We have decided to rewrite and not create Meru History for you, so that when we die, we might die "empty handed" that is, without carrying all our knowledge into our graves. Be blessed as you continue reading.

S/No.	Age group Group A	Year Circ.	Age group Group B	Year Circu.
1	Mbaine 3*	1713	Ntangi 3*	1723
	Kobia	1716	Kobia	1726
	Kaberia	1720	Kaberia	1730
2	Nkuthuku	1733	Mukuruma	1745
	Kobia	1738	Kobia	1750
	Kaberia	1742	Kaberia	1754
3	Ithalie	1757	Michubu	1769
	Kobia	1762	Kobia	1774
	Kaberia	1766	Kaberia	1777
4	Ratanya	1779	Githangiri	1790
	Kobia	1784	Kobia	1795
	Kaberia	1788	Kaberia	1798
5	Mbaringu	1799	Nguthugua	1809
	Kobia	1804	Kobia	1814
	Kaberia	1807	Kaberia	1818

6	Mbarata	1820	Kiruja	1831
	Kobia	1825	Kobia	1835
	Kaberia	1829	Kaberia	1839
7	Thambura	1842*	Nturitimi	1853
	Kobia	1847	Kobia	1859
	Kaberia	1851	Kaberia	1864
8	Kubai	1867	Guantai	1879
	Kobia	1871	Kobia	1883
	Kaberia	1876	Kaberia	1888
9	Gichunge	1891	Kiramunya	1906
	Kobia	1896	Kobia	1910
	Kaberia	1903	Kaberia	1914
10	Ithalie	1918	Michubu	1933
	Kobia	1924	Kobia	1939
	Kaberia	1928	Kaberia	1942
11	Ratanya	1947	Lubetaa	1961
	Kobia	1954	Kobia	1965
	Kaberia	1957	Kaberia	1969

12	Miriti	1972	Guantai	1985
	Kobia	1977	Kobia	1990
	Kaberia	1982	Kaberia	1995
13	Gichunge	1998	Kiramunya	2008
	Kobia	2002	Kobia	2011
	Kaberia	2006	Kaberia	2015
14	Ithalie	2018	Michubu	2027
	Kobia	2021	Kobia	2030
	Kaberia	2024	Kaberia	2033
15	Ratanya	2036	Lubetaa	2045
	Kobia	2039	Kobia	2048
	Kaberia	2042	Kaberia	2051
16	Miriti	2054	Guantai	2063
	Kobia	2057	Kobia	2066
	Kaberia	2060	Kaberia	2069
17	Kiramana	2072	Kaburia	2081
	Kobia	2075	Kobia	2084
	Kaberia	2078	Kaberia	2087

18	Ithalie	2090	Michubu	2099	
	Kobia	2093	Kobia	2102	
	Kaberia	2096	Kaberia	2105	
19	Ratanya	2108	Michubu	2117	INTERPRETATION OF THE TABLE
	Kobia	2111	Kobia	2120	
	Kaberia	2114	Kaberia	2123	
20	Miriti	2126	Guantai	2135	
	Kobia	2129	Kobia	2138	
	Kaberia	2132	Kaberia	2141	
21	Gichunge	2143	Guantai	2151	
	Kobia	2146	Kobia	2154	
	Kaberia	2149	Kaberia	2157	In the above table
22	Ithalie	2159	Michubu	2167	
	Kobia	2162	Kobia	2170	
	Kaberia	2165	Kaberia	2173	

or calendar, we have omitted the name Nding'uri immediately in the second column against every numerical number 1 to 22 and beyond, where we have inserted the age groups' names instead of Nding'uri. Therefore, the reader is advised to shift all the names directly following the numerical number to below the number and replace the same with Nding'uri, so that in the second column he will have simultaneous reading as age group of 1 is Mbaine, with Nding'uri, Kobia, Kaberia as its age sets, or 17 is Kiramana, with Nding'uri, Kobia, and Kaberia as its age sets and so on.

Long ago, the circumcision intervals were unpredictable because of many factors in life. Hunger and famine were most common factors that interfered with the intervals of circumcisions. Famine and hunger delayed circumcisions while war and serious raids postponed circumcisions until the security had been restored in the communities. That is why you will notice some longer intervals within the table above.

Factually and accurately, the several above columns

Should read in full where every Age group had three age sets named Nding'uri, Kobia and Kaberia. Remember that there was the first and the second Age group. The first was Mbaine and the second was

Ntangi, both were the sons of one man who allowed them to circumcise their sons in turns because they belonged to two different age groups according to their maturity ages.

BRIEF EXPLANATION

Remember, Ameru had left Egypt around and before AD 800, where they were the most advanced people who were expert Pyramids (Mbiira) or graves builders. Thereafter, they were forced out by the Libyan Mercenaries and the Assyrians who had invaded Egypt with the "force of the sword" to convert other people into Islam. In Kenya, not many communities are able to account for that Epoch in history.

There is also another Epoch of Ameru, detailing their epic journey from Egypt to Mboa through the wilderness of Nubia through Congo and Rwanda and Tanzania to Kenya.

Ameru arrived in Mboa (Manda Island) Kenya, around AD 1000, and that is where they lived up to the day when they were disturbed by Nguuntune (the Portuguese) who hunted and captured them as slaves from around AD 1500. When Ameru lived in Manda Island (Mboa) Kenya, they developed their customs, culture and traditions which they had almost forgotten while on their epic journey from Egypt. The Portuguese (Nguuntune) disturbed them when they captured them as slaves for export to Americas. That is another Epoch of Ameru in history because Ameru were not born or created in Meru. Ameru have a long history unlike many other communities in Kenya.

Before they escaped from Manda Island, they had been hunted earlier by Arabs as slaves for export into the Oceanic Islands of Tonga, Tuvalu, Samoa, Kiribati, Nauru, Vanuatu, Fiji, Niue, Papua and Palau in the Pacific Ocean. Ameru's life in Manda Island is another Epoch in their history where they advanced in farming and keeping of livestock.

Ameru escaped from Manda Island and arrived in the wilderness of what is now Meru National Park where they lived up to AD 1670. It was after that they commenced circumcision of their third Age Groups of Mbaine and Ntangi. Mbaine 1 and 2, including Ntangi 1 and 2 were all duly circumcised while they meandered in the wilderness of Bura,

Kora, Tulla and Bisannadi before arriving in Murera Grasslands (today Meru National Park). Ameru's life in the wilderness is another interesting Epoch in their history.

*3 on Mbaine and Ntangi indicates that there were previous two similar age groups that had been circumcised before 1700's while they lived in the wilderness of Bura, Kora,Tulla and Bisannadi before reaching the periphery of Merulands in early 18th, century. Ameru have the richest history among the communities of Kenya.

5.2 MEANING OF NAMES BURA, KORA AND TULLA ARE KIMERU NAMES EVEN TODAY NEAR MERU

Remember that Europeans and especially the British and German Colonizers forced their way into Africa in AD 1880's through the October 1886 Berlin Conference (termed Scramble for Africa) solely to save Africa from the Slave Trade Exploitation by Arabs, Portuguese and their allies in the Slave Trade that had been abolished in America in 1807 yet it continued and existed in Africa up to 1870's. But despite the abolition, slave traders were still supplying slaves in the background because some states had not effected the abolition order in America. The last states to abolish slavery in America did it in 1833 and 1848, though slave deals went on behind the scenes up to 1890's.

Therefore, the Nguuntune (Portuguese) and their allies chased and pursued slaves in Kenya interlands up to 1840's just before the arrival of the colonizers. That is, my great, great grandfather of Thambura age group who was born in 1820 and who was circumcised in 1842 must have witnessed slavery in action. Therefore, the story I got from my father from his father and from his grandfather who is my great, great grandfather must be accurate and vivid to the one who narrated the same to the writer. That story goes this way from the tellers.

WHEN Ameru left Mboa (Manda Island) in Kenya, they meandered in the wilderness of Bura, Kora, Tulla and Bisannadi (We are finished now by wild animals) for nearly a century before arriving in Meru. In-between Mboa and Meru, they went through the vast lands, grasslands, woodlands and the wilderness where they encountered wild animals which sometimes killed many people because they had exhausted their hunting tools on their long journey.

First they arrived in the grasslands where it rained very heavily in that particular season and as a result of heavy rains they named the place Mbura, but those who came afterwards called the place Bura. If you ask the present residents the meaning of Bura, they will never tell you, but "Mbura" corrupted Bura is a Kimeru name meaning heavy rains.

That is how the place acquired its name from Ameru who crossed the wilderness in 17th, century on their way to Merulands. The story continues, when Ameru continued with their journey towards Merulands, they came to a place where they encountered various types of wild animals in the thick wilderness where they got lost and they could not trace their bearings because of the wild animals. In that confusion, they said, "Tukuura, that is, we are lost." Those who occupied the wilderness later named the place Koora (kuura, get lost) corrupting the Kimeru name "Tukuura" for Koora. Kora or Kuura is a Kimeru name that was left by Ameru in their enroute to Meruland in 17th, century.

Today, it is Kora National Reserve in Tana River County. Ameru had crisscrossed that wilderness to find their bearing to Merulands in 17th, century. Also it was in Koora where they discovered "tan-oak-tree shoes" after their shoes had all been worn out in the long journey from Mboa. In that wilderness, they made their shoes out of the tan-oak-tree bark.

Finally, when Ameru arrived in the periphery of Merulands, they got tired and decided not travel any more. They thought that they had reached the end of their journey when they almost despaired and gave up by saying, "Tuutulla, we have reached the end, The Itulli or Final End." They lived in Tulla wilderness for some decades before proceeding to Murera country (the rich and fertile lands which yielded food for the community and hence Murera, the feeding ground) past Tulla and Bisannadi wastelands. Thus, Tulla in Kimeru meant the end of their long journey from Mboa. They decided to settle there until they were disturbed by teaming wild animals in Bisannadi and Murera Country of the Wildlife (Meru National Park) in Meru.

Those who narrated the story were born and lived in 1800's and for sure they had seen "Malimalimu" the

Arabs (hunters of slaves) who captured the people for sale and auction to the Nguuntune (the Portuguese) as slaves for export to America. The Arabs were branded Malimalimu because when they captured a soul, that soul never ever reappeared back in the village again. The captives disappeared forever and never to be seen again in the villages.

The captives went missing for life through "Malimalimu captors" who went to retail them for export to Americas. Although they had been hunted earlier as salves, that time, they were hunted in greater numbers because more slaves were required in Americas compared to elsewhere in the past.

The story of slavery is not old as many people visualize it to be. It is as fresh as you can pay attention to the stories of your great grandfathers who are living in 2021. As we edit this book, there are many people alive who were born in 1920's and they are great grandfathers, but most people are not interested in listening to them for good stories by enquiring from them. If you are a good reader, please make an effort to create a story by enquiry from your old relatives and that is how you will be an Historian who may add value to the history of Ameru in future.

CHAPTER SIX

6.0 HOW TRIBALISM WAS CONFIRMED IN KENYA

When Jomo Kenyatta appointed his first Cabinet, no one raised a finger about the persons who were appointed as Cabinet Ministers to head the Government Ministries and Departments. Jomo Kenyatta rewarded his acquiaintances and friends. It is by cheer luck that most of the tribes were represented in that Cabinet. At the time, politicians were moderate, reasonable, modest, sensible, restrained, judicious, unemotional, nonaggressive, reserved, impassive, thoughtful and no-nonsense in conduct of their duty performance. Cabinet Ministers never represented any tribe and they were appointed on pure merit and virtue to serve the communities equally. People never talked of their Ministers in the Cabinet because Ministers belonged to a fair Government that served communities equally.

Cabinet Ministers were men of honor, integrity and decency in their duty performance. They served the communities regardless of their backgrounds or where they came from and therefore, no one was interested or bothered to know how Jomo Kenyatta had picked the members of his Cabinet because he appointed them according to their expertise and merit. In those days, Cabinet Ministers were appointed on merit, expertise, virtue, proficiency, excellence and fitness to perform the functions of the departments allocated to them as a duty to serve communities in Kenya.

On the same note, Cabinet Ministers were reliable and dependable in their promises to the communities they served. They never gave false promises to the communities who expected their services. From the Cabinet Minister, every part of Kenya expected to enjoy the services of his departments equally. Every corner of the country felt the weight of good things from the functions of the Government Departments equally under meticulous and committed Cabinet Ministers who were faithful servants of the people.

Today, politicians demand services from the Cabinet Ministers for their communities despite the fact that they have a heavy Kitty known as the CDF at their disposal. Politicians aspire to grab everything they come across for "their people" who elected them and gave them power to make noise in their respective assemblies. They not only grab anything they come across with, but they also steal the funds from the Kitty meant for the people's development projects. Politicians demand more on behalf of the people but the more they get, the more they have to steal from the people. The bigger the cake, the bigger their slice of the cake. When politicians make noise, it is usually for their own benefits and not for the people they represent. That is, they fight for their own rights and not for their people, of whom they shout, "my people, my people, my people!"

Currently, they are politicians who have confirmed tribalism through dishonest "demands for their people." They use words like, "my people" as if they own people and go ahead to call the same people "marginalized" without specifying who marginalized them. They forget the fact that they are themselves who marginalize people by stealing from them. Instead of calling people who reside in their constituency, "my constituents" they call them "my people," including the elites who are better off in status in life. It is a mistaken comparison in life and that mistake impels them to steal from the public coffers in order to improve their status in life. Unfortunately only a few "well-to-do" and honest people join politics; majority are the poor. If the well-to-do and honest people joined politics and were genuinely committed to eradicate corruption, corruption would be diminished if not eradicated. But the fact is that only hungry people are ever interested in politics, their hunger will never allow them to pass harsh laws that punish thieves of public funds or other people involved in economic crimes. Politicians are ever thirsty and will always remain hungry people!

Tribalism was confirmed in Kenya when people from different regions thoughtlessly and imprudently started defending thieves from their regions and communities under the pretext that some criminals were being pursued as people from a particular tribe or a community was being targeted for this or that.

That is, whenever a thief was caught stealing, he cried wolf, "our people are being finished or our tribe is being finished." After that public outcry, the matter was politicized and the prosecuting agencies went slow in the matter of prosecution. From that time, tribalism was embraced by Kenyans and it was used as a tool to protect corrupt people in Kenya. That is how tribalism was confirmed in Kenya.

It was only after many years that people started to realize that tribalism had made it possible for some individuals to be leaders in Kenya. Kenyans realized that their leaders had come from two tribes in Kenya since Independence. When the third tribe wanted to lead the country, the two tribes that had produced Presidents took the advantage to confuse Kenyan masses by claiming personal misunderstanding to the extent that leaders would go ahead to pronounce that some tribes had produced many of the Presidents in the past. That claim was from the highest clones of leadership in the country. When leaders claim tribalism, who is capable of denying it? That way tribalism was confirmed in Kenya. Now, in the presence of tribalism in Kenya, people will never elect honest and meritorious leaders who are capable of serving the communities without bias and prejudice.

For Kenyans to disconnect themselves from the corruption that is conveyed up and bred in their communities by the individual beneficiaries in the name of leaders, Kenyans must think afresh. Those people who call the communities "their people" must stop doing so and embrace the call to unite people regardless of who they are in the regions, counties, sub-counties or locations. People who speak in name of the people branding them "my people" should stop that boring habit of ignorance. Instead of focusing on development for the people, they focus on people who need development that is supposed to be brought through funds which they steal as soon as funds are released from the National Treasury.

Tribalism is brought up and bred by some leaders who keep on blaming the Government for deficiencies that are caused by their own failures to implement the projects which fail to take off after they steal and misappropriate the funds allocated to them. Such leaders keep on speaking ill of the Government as if Government were foreign to them or as if they were not part of that Government.

Even masses are to blame, they elect people who promise them a good fight against the Government if they are elected and as if the Government was an antagonist. Their slogans are "If you elect me, I will ensure that the Government will do this and that for you because so and so, was not courageous enough to do this and that!" Instead of focusing on theft or misuse of the public funds that disappear into their hands, they focus on how they will deal with the Government and running away from the Government as if it were an enemy.

6.1 POLITICIANS CRAFTINESS IN DEALS

Politicians have become crafty people these days. They are stealing every right from the communities including the right to amend the Constitution. Recently two Kenyans whose families had been at loggerheads since Kenya's Independence days, decided to mend their fences after a second thought. They secretly decided to sit down and agree on how they should amend their fences and publicly shake their hands to prove to the Kenyans their friendship. Some people believed them and others never believed them because they were excluded from the talks that resulted in Great Handshake of warring leaders in Kenya.

The unknown terms of the handshake became an issue. People have wanted to know the conditions or terms of the handshake for some years from 9th, March 2018. The two individuals who conducted the handshake on their own behalf or on behalf of the people were not ready to divulge the contents of their discussions and terms for agreement.

What followed was the topic of their discussion that was titled "BBI" that was, Building Bridges Initiative. The question by an ordinary citizen was, "Whose bridges were those that had been broken?" Were they public or private bridges? People have taken upon themselves to interpret and answer questions to themselves without any conclusions.

People assume that the broken bridges by the two individuals affect public performance of their duties. The BBI issue which is the product of their personal agreement (handshake) concerned the Constitutional amendment. The pertinent question will forever remain in people's minds, "Can two warring individuals sit down and amend the

Constitution of the people by the people for the people?"

That question will never be answered by any clever intelligent person directly. The answer is "No" and it depends from whom it comes from. In the first place, when two warring people stop to fight and make peace for themselves, you cannot assume that they would discuss the fate of others positively. They will likely backbite someone in their discussion as a scapegoat for their quarrels, and that is why their discussion will remain secret.

From that point the public will say, "Two individuals cannot amend the Constitution." No matter their ranks or positions in life, they cannot amend the Constitution of the people by the people for the people, unless they are dictators of the people. Only dictators amend Constitutions to favor themselves so as to remain in power indefinitely.

For the Constitution to be amended, the process must be "people-driven." It is only Parliament that can introduce a motion in the Assembly to amend the Constitution and when the motion passes through its normal procedures of the Assembly, it is passed into the people who are represented by the

Assembly members to go through a Referendum. Judiciary and the executive have no power to initiate a motion to go through a Referendum because they are not representatives of the people. It is only Parliament that can initiate a motion in its House to amend the Constitution as people's representatives.

Institutions are not "people-driven" and therefore, Judiciary and Executive are pure institutions of the Government which cannot on their own initiate the amendment of the Constitution without a Referendum initiated through a motion in Parliament. Therefore, when two individuals sit down and suggest the amendment of Kenyan Constitution, people are quick to think that the country is in a state of calamity, where there is poverty, run away corruption, crumbling of the organizations and institutions and lack of checks and balances with declining standards of development in all sectors of the economy.

However, for now Kenya has not reached that stage of inability to think for itself. Thinkers were alert to the machinations and maneuvers being experienced in 2021 for the 2022 General Elections. The question of the BBI and its outcomes is very interesting. One will wonder who actually sponsored the motion or the suggestion that the Constitution be amended.

For one, the Government had a hand in the BBI report through an executive order that formed the Commission that projected the BBI report which suggested the Constitutional amendment. As far as our knowledge can guide us, No single arm of Government has that mandate. Even Parliament has no such power of amending the Constitution, leave alone a Commission formed by an Executive arm of the Government. It is the people's right and all legislators in Parliament are part and parcel of the government of the day.

The standing procedure for changing the Constitution is very clear. Parliament can bring and discuss a motion in the House. If the motion passes through all its stages it is taken to the people who are represented by the Assembly members in Parliament for the Referendum. Referendum is the right channel and route to change the Constitution; any other route is illegal in all its suggestions and directives. If BBI route to change the Constitution of Kenya were to go through, Kenya would have planted the seeds of dictatorship from 2021 that wouldl germinate after 2022 General Elections. Those words were from a stupid observer from the Utopia. Who is to believe a stupid person anyway? But they have followers too!

6.2 BEYOND TRIBALISM THINKING BY KENYANS

Kenyans are amusing people because they think beyond their Kenyan tribe or race. It is funny when one thinks about other people who live beyond Kenya like the Qataris wanting to lease farming land in Kenya way back in August 2009.

There is a funny story of unwarranted jealousy by a Kenyan in Kenyan National Assembly where in august house (Source August 6th, 1999), when the MP for Kangundo) seriously opposed the leasing of idle land at the Kenyan Coast to Qataris by the Government for farming in order to produce food and transfer farming technology to Kenyans. The concerned MP argued that the Government through the National Youth Service, had enough resources to farm on the land and boost food production in the country. The MP argued that the "4,000 inmates" spared death sentence by the President were enough to provide labor on that land intended for leasing to Qataris.

The story is funny because the MP's ability to stop leasing was prompt and immediate because in Kenya negative arguments and politics take priority from idle people who never realize what is good for those who would benefit from good Government projects. After the MP's stoppage to lease the idle land to Qataris, he never pursued or convinced the Government to use the idle labor of "4,000" prisoners who even today live idly to eat and drink from the taxpayers' sweat. His idea was very good but his jealousy has never produced any tin of beans from the idle land as the funny and jealous man intended. That is also how Kenyans curtailed Harambee Spirit!

One can imagine how Qataris would have transformed the idle land and transferred farming technology in Kenya since 2009! But murderers of the Harambee Spirit had their way to throw words of stagnation in the country. In 2022, that land still remains idle!

On 20th, July 2021, at 10:00 pm, Citizen TV hosted a serious debate in politics pitting two politicians from

Mathira and Ndaragwa Constituencies of Central Province. Their discussion was very healthy in balancing issues about two opposing Parties (Jubilee of the President of Kenya and UDA of the Deputy President of Kenya). Kenya has become mature politically where people are seen in the same village debating characters (behavior of the people) and not individuals as was the case in the past. It is interesting how a President can tolerate his deviant Deputy because the Constitution does not provide a procedure or a clue of what the President can do under those circumstances. People so far have not noted or learnt something about that weakness of the Constitution! The President has no absolute power and that is why he cannot dismiss his deviant Deputy because the good Constitution cannot allow it to happen. Why? A good question to be answered later.

Democracy is seen at work because the President says this and his Deputy shouts that without any repercussions. The only mistake is that Government is not seen to take up any responsibility because of the divided responsibility. So far citizens seem to enjoy because the President has his followers and the Deputy has his followers. Anyway who has no followers? Even KaMCA in the village has his followers because he can always shout, my people, my people!

In that situation, the masses suffer the consequences of their payukaring and bickering because nobody will ever believe them. In the process the economy will suffer and people will live to regret why they elected such people to lead them. Today, people cannot believe who is telling the truth in their midsts.

One wonders why Jomo Kenyatta, Daniel arap Moi and Mwai Kibaki in their total mature respective ages managed to lead people in Kenya successfully, while people who took up leadership at reasonable mature age are leading people to demean the Presidency, even to the point of mocking the Presidency. If democracy is meant to demean the Presidency, it should also be curtailed for its excesses by the young people who have never tasted the oppression by the oppressors.

In Kenya, when youth took leadership of the country, everyone was happy. In the first term of Uhuru Kenyatta Presidency, performance was admirable. But young people messed the Presidency in the second term because many young people wanted everything their way. In the hope of satisfying young people, many things went out of good hands which had performed well in the first term of the Presidency.

Trusting young blood in leadership has taught Kenyans a good lesson in politics. Kenyans must elect mature leaders in 2022. It is one century since when Italians allowed young blood to share leadership only to regret two decades later. Benito Mussolini edged his way into the Government in Italy as a "young tuck" when he became the Prime Minister of Italy only for the Italians to regret two decades later. Kenya should be aware of such mistakes in future! That is our advice.

Those aspiring for leadership in Kenya are all mature, except a few who want to test the depth of waters!

Printed in Great Britain
by Amazon